BACKHOES

A First Look

ZELDA WAGNER

Lerner Publications ◆ Minneapolis

Educator Toolbox

Reading books is a great way for kids to express what they're interested in. Before reading this title, ask the reader these questions:

> What do you think this book is about? Look at the cover for clues.
>
> What do you already know about backhoes?
>
> What do you want to learn about backhoes?

Let's Read Together

Encourage the reader to use the pictures to understand the text.

Point out when the reader successfully sounds out a word.

Praise the reader for recognizing sight words such as *have* and *they.*

TABLE OF CONTENTS

Backhoes

Backhoes dig up dirt.

Workers use backhoes to move and dump dirt.

Backhoes have a small bucket. It digs holes and dumps dirt.

Backhoes also have a bigger bucket.

What else could it pick up?

It picks up dirt. Then it moves dirt away.

A driver sits in the cab. The seat spins.

Why does the seat need to spin?

UPM-TAMAN PERTANIAN UNIVERSITI
KOMATSU
VAB 4287
UMW
WB
KOMATSU

An arm moves the small bucket.

Backhoes can dig deep holes. They can dig a pool!

What else could a backhoe dig a hole for?

Backhoes dig a long hole. Workers put in pipes.

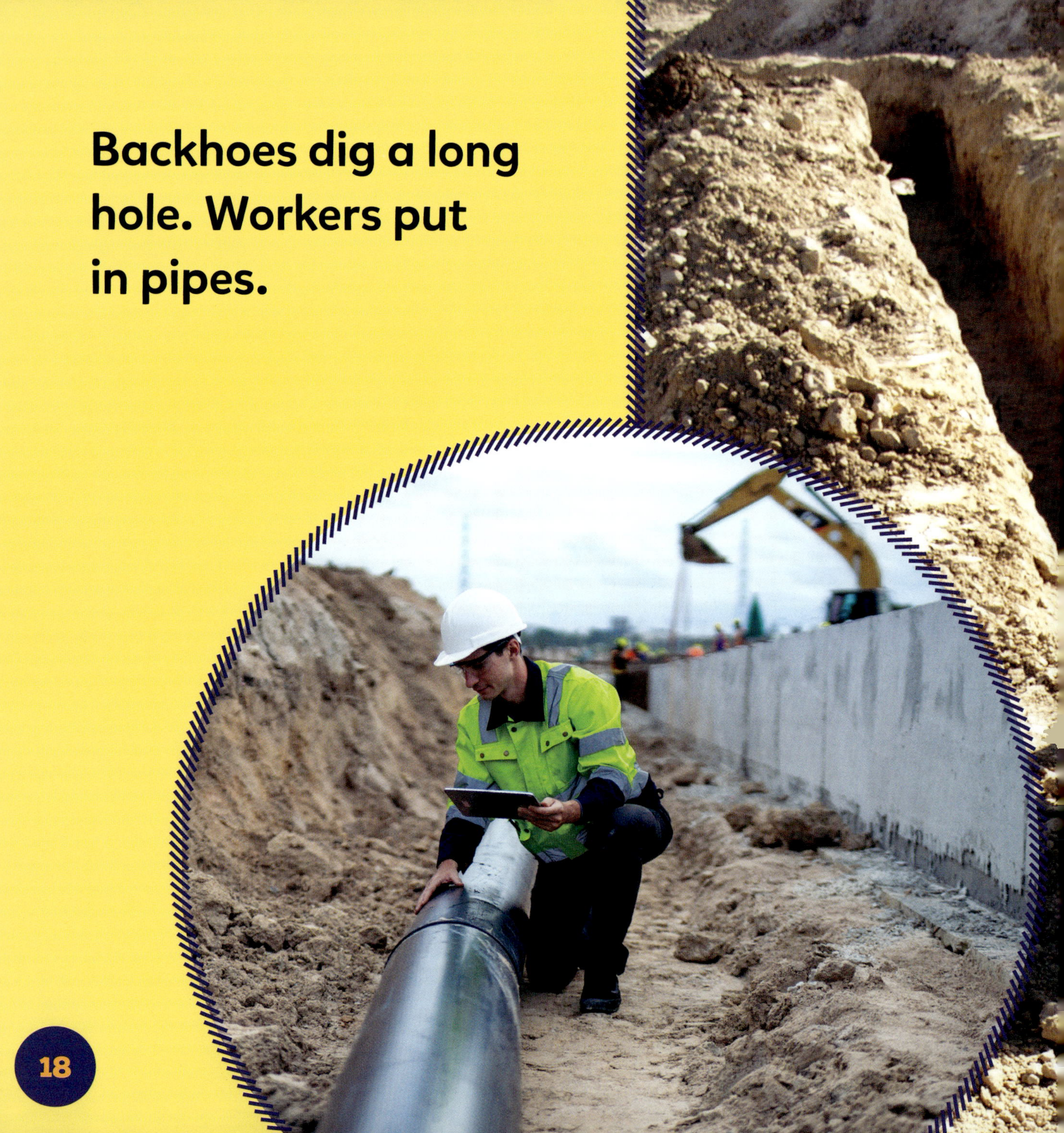

Backhoes do big jobs!

You Connect!

Have you ever seen a backhoe?

Would you want to drive a backhoe?

How can you learn more about backhoes?

STEM Snapshot

Encourage students to think and ask questions like scientists. Ask the reader:

What is something you learned about backhoes?

What is something you noticed about backhoe parts?

What is something you still want to learn about backhoes?

Photo Glossary

Learn More

Bolte, Mari. *Backhoes*. Mankato, MN: Creative Education and Creative Paperbacks, 2024.

Pettiford, Rebecca. *Backhoes*. Minneapolis: Jump!, 2023.

Wagner, Zelda. *Dump Trucks: A First Look*. Minneapolis: Lerner Publications, 2025.

Index

Photo Acknowledgments

Image credits: Jacquelin Grant/Alamy, pp. 4–5; Dmitry Kalinovsky/Shutterstock, pp. 6–7, 11; damircudic/Getty Images, p. 6 (bottom); Attapon Thana/Shutterstock, pp. 8–9; Anthony Pleva/Alamy, p. 10; Frank Paul/Alamy, pp. 12–13; adeqare/Shutterstock, pp. 14–15; Aleksandr Papichev/Alamy, pp. 16–17; Vithun Khamsong/Getty Images, p. 18; MICHELANGELOBOY/Getty Images, p. 19; Chet_W/Getty Images, p. 20.
Cover image: Dmitry Kalinovsky/Shutterstock.

Lerner Publications Company
An imprint of Lerner Publishing Group, Inc.
241 First Avenue North
Minneapolis, MN 55401 USA

For reading levels and more information, look up this title at www.lernerbooks.com.

Main body text set in Mikado Medium.
Typeface provided by Hannes von Doehren.

Lerner team: Martha Kranes

Library of Congress Cataloging-in-Publication Data

Names: Wagner, Zelda, 2000- author.
Title: Backhoes : a first look / Zelda Wagner.
Description: Minneapolis : Lerner Publications, [2025] | Series: Read about construction vehicles | Includes bibliographical references and index. | Audience: Ages 5–8 | Audience: Grades K–1 | Summary: "Backhoes do big jobs! Construction workers use them to dig and carry away dirt. With large, colorful photos and reader questions, young readers will enjoy learning more about backhoes and what they do"— Provided by publisher.
Identifiers: LCCN 2024006448 (print) | LCCN 2024006449 (ebook) | ISBN 9798765647806 (library binding) | ISBN 9798765657119 (epub)
Subjects: LCSH: Backhoes—Juvenile literature.
Classification: LCC TA735 .W34 2025 (print) | LCC TA735 (ebook) | DDC 621.8/65—dc23/eng/20240315

LC record available at https://lccn.loc.gov/2024006448
LC ebook record available at https://lccn.loc.gov/2024006449

ISBN 979-8-7656-6218-2 (pbk.)

Manufactured in the United States of America
1-1010886-53341-4/8/2024